MEETING JESUS

The 'I Am' Sayings of Christ

CW00550487

MEETING JESUS

The 'I Am' Sayings of Christ

R. C. Sproul

'He said to them, "But who do *you* say that I am?"'
MATTHEW 16:15

THE BANNER OF TRUTH TRUST

THE BANNER OF TRUTH TRUST

Head Office
3 Murrayfield Road
Edinburgh
EH12 6EL
UK

North America Office
PO Box 621
Carlisle
PA 17013
USA

banneroftruth.org

Adapted from the video teaching series
Knowing Christ: The 'I Am' Sayings of Jesus,
published by Ligonier Ministries.
This edition © The R. C. Sproul Trust 2019

*

ISBN
Print: 978 1 84871 928 6
EPUB: 978 1 84871 929 3
Kindle: 978 1 84871 930 9

*

Typeset in 11/15 Adobe Garamond Pro
at The Banner of Truth Trust, Edinburgh

Printed in the USA by
Versa Press Inc.,
East Peoria, IL.

Contents

CHAPTER ONE

The Bread of Life

Who is Jesus? Nearly every adult person has formed some opinion of Jesus. These opinions may be superficial, uninformed, or downright heretical. When Jesus met with his disciples at Caesarea Philippi, he asked them, 'Who do people say that the Son of Man is?' (Matt. 16:13). In response, his disciples gave a report of the rumours circulating around the countryside. Then he turned back to the disciples and asked, 'But who do you say that I am?' It is here that Simon Peter gives the confession, 'You are the Christ, the Son of the living God' (verse 16). Jesus responded, 'Blessed are you, Simon Bar-Jonah, for flesh and blood has not revealed this to you, but My Father who is in heaven' (verse 17).

The church of Jesus Christ is a confessing church. When we speak of the church as a confessing church, we're not simply speaking of the confession of sin. Rather, we're speaking with respect to the confession of our faith – that

Christ promises redemption to those who believe him in their hearts and confess him with their mouths (Rom. 10:9). The confession of faith upon which the church was established was a confession that focused on Jesus Christ. The truth about Jesus – not mere opinion – matters, and it matters eternally. This truth about Jesus is communicated especially through his 'I am' sayings.

Manna from heaven

The first 'I am' saying of Jesus is, 'I am the bread of life.' In John 6:30 we read: 'So they said to him, "Then what sign do you do, that we may see and believe you? What work do you perform?"' The people are asking for some sign that will prove to them the truth of the claims that Jesus had been making about himself. They are recalling when God manifested his presence to the children of Israel in the wilderness by supernaturally providing food for them.

Jesus answers by saying, 'Truly, truly, I say to you, it was not Moses who gave you the bread from heaven, but my Father gives you the true bread from heaven. For the bread of God is he who comes down from heaven and gives life to the world' (verses 32-33). To which they replied, 'Sir, give us this bread always.' And Jesus said to them, 'I am the bread of life; whoever comes to me shall not hunger, and whoever believes in me shall never thirst.' This is the first 'I am' saying.

The extraordinary thing – not only in this 'I am' saying, but in all of them – is the structure of Jesus' statement.

Normally when someone wants to say 'I am' in Greek, they would use the first person singular form of the verb 'to be' which is the word *eimi*. However, what is strange about this particular statement of Jesus is that he doesn't say, '*Eimi* (I am) the bread of life.' Rather, he adds another word, the Greek personal pronoun *egō,* and says, '*Egō eimi* the bread of life.' To the Greek hearer it sounds like a redundancy or a stutter, because Jesus is literally saying, 'I, I am the bread of life.'

What makes this significant is that the structure of the sentence is exceedingly rare. One of the important places we find it used in this way is in the Septuagint, which is the Greek translation of the Old Testament. In this translation, when God reveals his name to Moses in the burning bush, he says, 'I AM WHO I AM' (Exod. 3:14). The way in which that phrase is used by God to reveal himself is rendered by this exact form, '*Egō eimi.*' There is, then, a thinly veiled reference back to the sacred name of God when Jesus refers to himself with this language, '*Egō eimi.*'

Jesus said to his contemporaries, in referring back to the manna of the Old Testament, that Moses did not provide the manna in the wilderness. When the manna was given Moses was only the mediator of God's covenant people, Israel. Though Moses announced that the manna would be given, he wasn't the one who provided it. It was God who sent the manna; it came from heaven. Therefore, it is critical for Jesus to identify himself with this same kind of provision that God gave in the Old Testament. When Jesus proclaims this truth, he's speaking about his origin. This is the point that is vital for our own understanding of Jesus' self-consciousness. Jesus didn't say, 'I come from Bethlehem,' or, 'I come from Nazareth.' Rather, he says, 'I come from heaven. I am the one that the Father sent from heaven. I am the true bread, the bread that gives life to all who partake of it.'

Jesus' heavenly kingdom

The New Testament is deeply concerned about the exaltation of Christ after his death and resurrection, and about his entering into glory. At the heart of the concept of Christ's exaltation is his ascension into heaven. The word *ascension* does not simply mean 'going up somewhere.' When the New Testament speaks about the ascension of Jesus, it isn't simply referring to an elevated point to which Jesus goes. Instead, it speaks about Jesus going to a particular place for a particular reason. It is not just *an* ascension to heaven, but instead an ascension *to* a heavenly throne. In like manner, when the Scripture speaks of Jesus 'sitting' at the right hand of the Father, it isn't merely pointing out that Jesus is close to the Father. Rather the seat on which Jesus sits is the seat of authority. By his ascension, the New Testament refers to Jesus going to the right hand of the Father where he then has his coronation as the King of the kings and as the Lord of the lords.

Jesus does not, however, merely reign. He also serves in the heavenly realms as our true high priest. As the book of Hebrews emphasizes, Jesus is the greater priest, in part because, having been raised from the dead, his priesthood is forever. John Calvin described the scope of Christ's continuing ministry as a *munus triplex,* or 'threefold office' – he is our prophet, priest, and king. That is why Jesus can say, 'No one has ascended into heaven' (John 3:13).

However, Jesus is not saying that his people will not follow him in the resurrection. In fact, we Christians are all promised we will go up to heaven at the time of our death. He meant no one would ascend in the unique sense that he ascended to his place of cosmic authority. When he speaks of the uniqueness of his ascension, what does he say? 'No one has ascended into heaven except he who descended from heaven, the Son of Man' (3:13). In Jesus' understanding, his ascension is linked to his prior descension. When he ascends into heaven, he's simply returning to the place from whence he came.

In this, Jesus calls attention to his heavenly origin, saying that the place he came from was heaven itself. In like manner, just as it was the Father and not Moses who sent the manna, so it was the Father who sent the Son.

'All that the Father gives'

John chapter 6 has been a focal point of discussion with respect to the dependence of the believer upon the grace of God for salvation.

> Jesus said to them, 'I am the bread of life; whoever comes to
> me shall not hunger, and whoever believes in me shall never

thirst. But I said to you that you have seen me and yet do not believe. All that the Father gives me will come to me, and whoever comes to me I will never cast out. For I have come down from heaven, not to do my own will but the will of him who sent me. And this is the will of him who sent me, that I should lose nothing of all that he has given me, but raise it up on the last day. For this is the will of my Father, that everyone who looks on the Son and believes in him should have eternal life, and I will raise him up on the last day' (verses 35-40).

This chapter in general, and especially this passage, is brimming with the doctrine of predestination. It is interesting to see how many commentators, when they come to John 6, try to avoid this doctrine. At the heart of these sayings is Jesus' affirmation, which he repeats in his High Priestly Prayer in John 17, that there is a body of people that the New Testament calls *the elect*. Here, Jesus says that all whom the Father gives to him will come to him.

Every person that the Father gives to the Son comes to the Son, and all of those who come to the Son are never cast out. Instead they receive their nourishment from the one whom the Father sent on their behalf. They feed upon and are strengthened by the bread of life, which not only sustains us in our earthly existence, but also gives life everlasting. And just as with the statement of his origins, this claim caused great uproar and discussion.

Jesus addresses the people and says, 'Do not grumble among yourselves. No one can come to me unless the Father who sent me draws him' (John 6:43, 44). Twice in John 6, Jesus speaks about man's natural ability to respond to Jesus on his own. It is an assumption in mainstream evangelicalism that Jesus was sent into the world by God as a potential Saviour for everyone, and every individual in the world has the ability to come or not to come to Jesus. We struggle when Jesus himself says that nobody is able to come to him '*unless* …' The word *unless* underscores what we would call a necessary condition – a condition that must be met for a desired consequence or effect to occur. Jesus is teaching his hearers about the necessary condition of faith. He is telling them that they can't come to him and won't come to him, because they are dead in their sin. Faith is a gift granted by God. Some people believe God gives that gift to everyone, but remember Jesus says '*all*' that the Father gives to him will come to him. He reinforces this by saying, 'This is why I told you that no one can come to me unless it is granted him by the Father' (verse 65).

The drawing of God

Throughout church history, there has been debate over the significance, meaning, and application of the verb 'to draw,' that Jesus uses in verse 44. It is fascinating that 'to draw' is the common English translation. The same word is used in the book of Acts when people are thrown into prison. *The Theological Dictionary of the New Testament* translates the verb 'to draw' as 'to compel.' When we think of something being drawn, we usually think of it being enticed, wooed, or persuaded. So we could paraphrase this verse, 'Nobody can come to me unless the Father woos him, unless he entices him, unless he persuades him.'

In truth, the verb is much stronger than that. The wooing, the drawing that God does is fully effective. When God the Holy Spirit actively draws a person to Jesus, that person comes to Jesus. The person God draws to Jesus comes not because they are coerced or pulled kicking and screaming against their will but because God the Holy Spirit, in that act of effectual drawing, changes the heart of the person. We come willingly, even joyfully. Where that person previously was blind to the things of God, now the scales of the eyes have been removed. That which was unpleasant to the soul is now shown to be sweet, attractive and altogether desirable. The heavenly drawing of God is one by which the inner disposition of the soul is changed by God, so that when the Father draws someone to his Son, he comes to his Son. He eats the bread of life giving him spiritual life that is forever.

There is no other source for eternal life anywhere under heaven than in Christ himself.

CHAPTER TWO

The Light of the World

The second of the 'I am' sayings of Jesus is 'I am the light of the world' (John 8:12). Depending on the Bible version you use, this statement may be referenced in different places. In this passage we read, 'Again Jesus spoke to them, saying, "I am the light of the world. Whoever follows me will not walk in darkness, but will have the light of life."' What precedes this statement is the account of the woman caught in adultery. In fact, the subheading for John chapter 8 in the New King James Version is 'An Adulteress Faces the Light of the World.' In some ancient manuscripts this account does not occur at the beginning of chapter 8. For this reason, there is an ongoing discussion as to where it belongs in the text of the New Testament. There's virtually no argument that it is apostolic in origin, but there is disagreement as to where it fits in the narrative.

Often the surrounding context of an event helps us grasp the intended meaning. Whether or not this 'I am' belongs next to the account of the woman caught in adultery, however, doesn't change its essential meaning. The normal place we find it is in chapter 8, and so we will work on the assumption that Jesus gives this statement to the people after they have dragged this woman out of the darkness and made a public spectacle of her guilt; dragging her sin, as it were, into the light of day. After dismissing her accusers – accusing them by inviting the one without sin to cast the first stone – and granting his grace to her, Jesus says, 'I am the light of the world. Whoever follows me will not walk in darkness, but will have the light of life.'

The light from within

The term *light* is one of the most important terms in John's entire Gospel. For example, John uses the words *light*, *life*, and *truth* repeatedly. Of course, John's Gospel is not the only place in the New Testament we find light being used as a metaphor for the truth of the gospel, the ministry of Christ and for what happens to those who are converted to Christ. In our natural, fallen condition we are described as being children of the darkness. In this sense, the darkness refers to a moral deficiency or corruption of the human heart.

I can't help but be reminded of Joseph Conrad's classic novel, *Heart of Darkness*. A heart of darkness is a heart that lives in a state of corruption. We speak about works that are done in darkness. People who are engaged in virtuous deeds are not inclined to hide in dark places. The darkness is the place where unspeakable sins are carried out, concealed from public display. The Old Testament prophet Isaiah, when he gave his messianic prophecy of the one who would come – the servant of the Lord – wrote, 'The people who walked in darkness have seen a great light' (Isa. 9:2). Even the secular world uses this kind of language, describing what they conceive to be a great leap forward in learning as 'the Enlightenment' and the time preceding it as 'the Dark Ages.'

We see this antithesis between light and darkness throughout Scripture, beginning even in the creation account in Genesis – where God creates the light, separating it from the darkness. Jesus is the light of the world and radiates the refulgent glory of God himself because God is seen as being light. God is viewed as dwelling in light inaccessible, and he radiates the glory of his own character. When we see God manifesting himself in Scripture, he does it repeatedly with overpowering experiences of light. When Jesus appears to Saul on the road to Damascus, Saul is blinded with a light brighter than the noonday sun. This is seen on the Mount of Transfiguration, where the deity of Christ bursts through the veil of his humanity. His countenance changed, his clothes began to glow, and a brilliant light enveloped him so that the disciples fell on their face as though they were dead.

To grasp what occurs here it is important for us, in the first place, to understand the nature of colour. For example, if you were to examine an orange and were asked to describe the colour, you'd most likely respond, 'the orange is the colour orange.' But what colour would the orange be if the lights were turned off? It would be black, because the only time an orange is orange is when light reflects upon it. Without the source of light, everything is black – there is no colour. Purity of colour is found in light itself. I'm reminded of this every time I see a rainbow in the sky, where the prism of colour shows us the beauty found within light.

When the disciples recount the Transfiguration, in which the light of deity radiated from Christ, he was not reflecting it. Instead, the light was shining from *within* him. This is unlike Moses whose face shone after he had seen the back of God. Moses was shining with a reflected glory, not with an inherent or intrinsic glory. Christ, when he began to burst forth in this light at the Mount of Transfiguration, was displaying his own internal glory. This is why John writes in the opening of his Gospel, 'And the Word became flesh and dwelt among us, and we have seen his glory, glory as the only Son from the Father, full of grace and truth' (John 1:14).

Though it is not until chapter 8 that John records Jesus calling himself the light of the world, he is described in those terms earlier:

> In the beginning was the Word, and the Word was with God, and the Word was God. All things were made through him, and without him was not any thing made that was made. In him was life, and the life was the light of men.

The light shines in the darkness, and the darkness has not overcome it (John 1:1-5).

There's no passage in all of Scripture that more clearly affirms the deity of Christ than the prologue of John's Gospel. It says of the second person of the Trinity – the *Logos* – that he was with God in the beginning, that he was God from the beginning, and that he is the creator of all things. It says, 'In him was life, and the life was the light of men.' This is the light that shines in the darkness – the *Logos* himself. The ultimate light source was coming into the world and was not comprehended by the people of darkness. John's Gospel goes on to say, 'There was a man sent from God, whose name was John' (verse 6). This, of course, refers to John the Baptist. 'He came as a witness, to bear witness about the light, that all might believe through him. He was not the light, but came to bear witness about the light. The true light, which gives light to everyone, was coming into the world' (verses 7-9).

Light shows reality

This metaphor of light and darkness is found not simply in the New Testament or in Christian literature but is also found in other sources, such as in the ancient philosophers. It was certainly one of the favourite metaphors of the philosopher Plato. In *The Republic* Plato has a famous parable where he tells the story of slaves who are confined within a cave. There is a small fire going in the cave, but it is behind these men who are tied up, and the only light they have is a vague light that reflects shadows on the wall of the cave. These people believe, because it is all they can see, that the shadows are the only reality there is. What Plato calls these shadows dancing on the walls of the cave is 'opinion.' He understands these shadows as being less than true knowledge. In Plato's parable, he says that for a person to acquire true knowledge, they have to get out of the cave, out of the darkness and into the noonday sun where they can behold objects as they really are. It is only in the context of light that reality can be known – where you can have true knowledge. Everything else is simply dim approximation, just opinion that does not matter. This is a critical part of Plato's philosophy and emblematic of what he saw as his goal as a philosopher: to free men so they could rightly see reality.

Why is that significant to Christianity? In the second century, the Christian apologist Justin Martyr stated that not only do we find truth in the sources that God gives to us, but that the light of God's truth also shines through creation. Paul tells us in the first chapter of Romans that God's revelation comes not only in the Bible, but also through nature, where 'The heavens declare the glory of God, and the sky above proclaims his handiwork' (Psa. 19:1). Justin Martyr goes on to say that some people, even unbelievers, get some glimpse of reality. This is why unbelievers can be effective physicians, mathematicians, biologists, or whatever else, because they work with the light of nature and we should be grateful for this truth, as Christians glean great benefit from unbelievers. We can then step back and be impressed by the insights of Plato, Aristotle and Cicero. In the same way, we can be healed by an unbelieving doctor or travel on a plane designed by an unbelieving engineer. Any valuable knowledge found in Plato ultimately comes from the supreme source of light – Christ, the one who lights everyone who comes into the world. In other words, apart from the light of God's grace given to the world through Christ, there would be nothing but ignorance and darkness. Even those who are not Christians participate in some of the benefits coming from the light that has entered into the world. Even when people reject the light, they still partici-pate in benefits of the light.

The glory of the light

It is also important to realize, when we go back to the account of creation on the very first page of sacred Scrip-ture, we are told 'In the beginning, God created the heav-ens and the earth' (Gen. 1:1). And then we read, 'The earth was without form and void, and darkness was over the face of the deep' (1:2). The pre-structured universe which God describes in the first chapter of the Bible is, before his work of creation begins, formless and chaotic. All we have is emp-tiness and darkness.

Think of those three metaphors – formlessness, empti-ness and darkness. They are all negative, ominous-sounding words in our vocabulary, but what do we see in the very first act of creation? The Spirit hovers over the face of the deep and God says, 'Let there be light' (Gen. 1:3), and instantly the light comes on. The very first act God performs in creation is to bring light to a universe that is filled with darkness.

God himself is described in terms of light. That's the beginning of the biblical revelation. And when we go to the end of the biblical revelation, we read John's vivid description of the new heavens and the new earth in the final chapters of Revelation. John has a vision inside heaven, and sees the new Jerusalem descending from heaven. Describing the interior of the holy city, he says there is no light there – but why? Because the glory of God and the Lamb light the heavenly places. There is no night, because the presence of God radiates light constantly. That is what the Bible describes as the glory of God – the refulgence of his blazing purity and brightness comes to us in light.

All of this is contained in Jesus' claim 'I am the light of the world. Whoever follows me will not walk in darkness, but will have the light of life' (John 8:12). Isn't it interesting that when someone becomes converted, we use the expression, 'They've seen the light,' because previously they were blinded to the things of God? Religion seemed, before conversion, unnecessary, irrational, fanatical, and – above all – insignificant. Then, suddenly, when their eyes are opened and they see the full-orbed sweetness of Christ's radiance, everything changes.

Blind, but now I see

Another place where Jesus calls himself 'the light of the world' is in the context of his healing the man who was born blind. When the man opens his eyes for the first time, the first thing he sees is the very Light of the World who gave him his sight. When Jesus makes his claim to being the light of the world, see the response:

> So the Pharisees said to him, 'You are bearing witness about yourself; your testimony is not true.' Jesus answered, 'Even if I do bear witness about myself, my testimony is true, for I know where I came from and where I am going, but you do not know where I come from or where I am going. You judge according to the flesh; I judge no one. Yet even if I do judge, my judgment is true, for it is not I alone who judge, but I and the Father who sent me. In your Law it is written that the testimony of two people is true. I am the one who bears witness about myself, and the Father who sent me bears witness about me.' They said to him therefore, 'Where is your Father?' Jesus answered, 'You know neither me nor my Father. If you knew me, you would know my Father also' (John 8:13-19).

According to Jewish law, when testimony was given and claims were made, they had to be corroborated by another source in order for the testimony to be legal. It is necessary to have the agreement of at least two witnesses. Here Jesus says, 'I am the light of the world,' and the Pharisees in effect say: 'No, you're not. Nobody else is corroborating or verifying this stupendous claim you are making.' Jesus responds, 'I don't have to have any corroboration because I know who I am. I know where I came from and where I'm going.' This is an incredible statement. Just as he had done when he talked about being the bread of life, Jesus makes reference to his place of origin. When God speaks, you don't need human corroboration.

Instead, divine corroboration is found in different places within the New Testament. It can be found at the baptism of Jesus when the Father speaks audibly from heaven, 'This is my beloved Son, with whom I am well pleased' (Matt. 3:17). We see it again at Jesus' transfiguration when the Father says, 'This is my beloved Son, with whom I am well pleased; listen to him' (Matt. 17:5). And corroboration is found again in the third chapter of John's Gospel when Nicodemus comes to Jesus at night saying, 'Rabbi, we know that you are a teacher come from God, for no one can do these signs that you do unless God is with him' (John 3:2). Jesus' miracles and signs reflected God's attestation, confirmation, and corroboration of his claims.

CHAPTER THREE

The Door

We have already seen that when Jesus uses the 'I am' formula, his usage of the statement equates with the Old Testament language for God – 'Yahweh,' I AM THAT I AM. Now we are going to look at the statement that Jesus makes in chapter 10 of John's Gospel, 'I am the door' (verse 7). Before we look at that, however, it should be noted that Jesus expresses another important 'I am' saying in this passage when he calls himself 'the good shepherd' (verse 11). In the same context, Christ calls himself 'the door' and 'the good shepherd.' Those two expressions have to be distinguished from one another because they do not mean quite the same thing. But even though we distinguish between them, we must never separate them, as they are closely related to each other.

The first 'I am' saying Jesus expresses is the statement, 'I am the door.' The context for this saying begins where Jesus says:

'Truly, truly, I say to you, he who does not enter the sheep-fold by the door but climbs in by another way, that man is a thief and a robber. But he who enters by the door is the shepherd of the sheep. To him the gatekeeper opens. The sheep hear his voice, and he calls his own sheep by name and leads them out. When he has brought out all his own, he goes before them, and the sheep follow him, for they know his voice. A stranger they will not follow, but they will flee from him, for they do not know the voice of strangers.'

So Jesus again said to them, 'Truly, truly, I say to you, I am the door of the sheep. All who came before me are thieves and robbers, but the sheep did not listen to them. I am the door. If anyone enters by me, he will be saved and will go in and out and find pasture. The thief comes only to steal and kill and destroy. I came that they may have life and have it abundantly' (John 10:1-10).

Protecting the sheep

Here, in the beginning of the Good Shepherd Discourse, Jesus likens himself to the door of the sheepfold. There is a rich historical background that Jesus is crafting for his hearers. We know the shepherding vocation was important in the ancient Jewish community. The Old Testament is replete with references to shepherding. Moses served as a shepherd in the forty years between his exile from Egypt and his return there when he was used of God to free his people. David was the shepherd king of Israel and, of course, we are most familiar with Psalm 23 that refers to the Lord as the shepherd of his people.

In the ancient world, sheep grazed outside during the day. The shepherd led them beside the still waters and into the green pastures where they could be nourished by feeding in the pasture lands. If you have seen flocks of sheep, you know they move about haphazardly with no seeming rhyme or reason. Without a shepherd, they behave in a way that makes us believe they are foolish. This is why the shepherd was there to guide and protect the sheep of his flock.

At night, however, the sheep were brought in from the pasture and kept in a place that was protected, called the sheepfold. There were different kinds of sheepfolds. Some of them were made of wood with fencing to protect the interior, but more often the sheepfold was constructed of stone. It was an almost impregnable fortress to shelter and protect the sheep from thieves or wild animals that might harm the flock. The walls around the sheepfold didn't have barbed wire at the top (they didn't have barbed wire in those days), but they often had sharp thorns attached to discourage an intruder from trying to climb over the wall. That's why Jesus said that only those who were out for destruction, thievery, or murder would climb over the wall. The door was the proper way of entrance for the sheep and, most importantly, for the shepherd. One person within the sheepfold would often be in charge of guarding the door. He was not the shepherd, he was the guardian of the door. In some of the enclosures during Jesus' time, there was not so much a door as an opening into the fold. The opening would be wide enough for the sheep to enter and exit, and just wide enough for the guardian to lie down and sleep. That way, if anyone tried to enter through the 'door' – which literally was the guardian – he would be awakened to the danger.

Often the sheepfolds were big enough to contain several different flocks of sheep. Various shepherds would come in with their sheep at night. The sheep would not get lost and intermixed with the other flocks because the sheep recognized their shepherd, and the shepherd recognized his sheep. Don't lose sight however of this important truth: the entrance to the sheepfold, which is the place of protection, is the door. The first image that Jesus uses here in this context is the door—'I am the door.'

There are records of sheep farmers who can recognize their sheep by their distinctive markings and characterizations. Additionally, the shepherd, if he spent any time with his sheep and got to know them and they got to know him, could stand inside the sheepfold and call the sheep and they would come running, because—though they are supposedly foolish animals—they recognize the voice of their shepherd. Again, the only entrance into the sheepfold is through the door. The shepherd opens the door, the sheep hear his voice, and he calls his own sheep by name and leads them out. When he brings out his own sheep and exits the sheepfold, he goes first and leads them through the door to the grazing pastures, and the sheep follow him. Even before the story of the good shepherd, there is emphasis given concerning the behaviour of the sheep with respect to the good shepherd.

Too often as we read the New Testament, we start reading at the beginning of a particular chapter and we tend to think that what we are reading is an isolated incident disconnected from that which comes before it. The truth is that chapter 10 follows exactly on the heels of chapter 9 and since in the original Gospel there were no chapter or verse divisions, we must look at what immediately precedes chapter 10 to see what motivated Jesus to give this illustration.

The context in which Jesus made this statement was with respect to the healing of the man born blind, whom Jesus touched and enabled to see light for the first time. The Pharisees and the Sadducees were furious with Jesus for the claims he was making about himself, but they were also furious with the man who had been healed. They virtually excommunicated this poor man and, instead of rejoicing, the Pharisees were angry. Immediately after this confrontation with the Pharisees, Jesus introduces this saying about his being the door to the sheepfold, as well as the good shepherd. The Pharisees, who were called to be the shepherds of God's people, were instead like thieves and robbers who had no concern for the well-being of the sheep. Here a man born blind was under the Pharisees' pastoral care. He was a member of their flock. With these words it is as if Jesus were saying to them, 'What kind of shepherds are you? That's all the concern you have for your sheep? What have you ever done for this man, for this lamb of your flock? You are more concerned about your own status. You are more concerned about your own reputation than you are of the welfare of this man whom I have healed.' This is the context in which Jesus makes his statement about the door.

The door to God's kingdom

When Jesus talks about the sheepfold and the door to the sheepfold, he uses a common, earthly, real-life situation with which his audience would have been familiar to call attention to a higher truth. Remember, at the heart of Jesus' parables and illustrations is his communication about the kingdom of God. He frequently began telling a parable, 'The kingdom of God is like … .' What Jesus is saying is that God has a sheepfold, a place of sanctuary and safety. God has a place of everlasting peace and protection, where he himself is the mighty fortress for his people. And that fortress, like the sheepfold, has a door. As Jesus is here speaking about the kingdom and presence of God, he is expounding the glorious truth that he not only leads us there, but also keeps us there.

Jesus' teaching was offensive to the Pharisees, but I believe there is no time or culture in the history of the Christian church more offended by this kind of teaching than the one in which we live. If Jesus ever made a statement that was politically incorrect, it is this one. What Jesus is saying about himself is that the kingdom is exclusive, not inclusive, and the sheepfold does not have fifteen different doors and ways to enter. There is only one door and, as the New Testament repeats time and again, there is only one mediator between God and man – Christ himself. The flock of God has one shepherd and the only way into the sheepfold is through the one who is the door. That is offensive to the inclusive, pluralistic culture in which we live. Christians are frowned upon when they talk like this. However, we must remember that it is Jesus and the apostles who make this claim. Peter says, 'For there is no other name under heaven given among men by which we must be saved' (Acts 4:12).

When Jesus says, 'All who came before me are thieves and robbers,' to whom is he referring? It does not fit that he would be referring to the prophets of the Old Testament; and he is certainly not calling Moses or Isaiah a thief or a robber. He is instead referring to those who were false messiahs, who claimed to be the way to God. Our pluralistic culture claims there are many ways to God, insisting that it does not matter what you believe. Whether you are a Buddhist, Hindu or Taoist, it is taught that all roads lead to God. But this all-inclusive concept is on a direct collision course with what the Scriptures teach about salvation and Christ – that he is the *monogenēs*, 'the only begotten,' of the Father.

Jesus, the only way

My English professor at college was openly hostile to Christianity and one day she asked me in front of the whole class, 'Mr Sproul, do you think that Jesus is the only way to God?'

I felt the stares of everyone in the class. I knew I was in deep, deep trouble, because if I was to say, 'Yes,' then I would be a bigot. If I was to say, 'No,' I would be a traitor. So, I mumbled my answer.

She said, 'What did you say?'

I said, 'Yes, I think he is the only way.'

She attacked me, saying, 'That's the most arrogant, narrow-minded, bigoted statement I have ever heard.'

She humiliated me before the class and, when I left, I stopped at the door and calmly said to her, 'I know that you do not believe in Christianity, but do you think it is possible that a person can be truly persuaded that Jesus is at least one way to God?'

She said, 'Well, yes, of course.'

I said, 'Well, if someone is persuaded that Jesus is one way to God, and then he finds that the self-same Jesus says he is the *only* way to God, what is the person to do? If I thought Jesus was the only way to God because he happens to be my way and that you have to believe my way because only I have the truth, then of course, that would be arrogant, bigoted, and narrow-minded of me. If, however, I am persuaded Jesus is the Christ, and he teaches that he is the only way, do you not see that I would be betraying him if I said to make you happy or the culture happy that there are many ways?'

She said, 'Yes, I do see that. But I have to say, how can you believe in a God that only gives one way?'

I replied, 'Well, that is the thing that amazes me.'

She said, 'What?'

'That he gives a way. Why should he give any way? Think of what he has done, the extent to which he has gone to redeem a fallen world through the ministry of Christ, whose life and person is not worthy to be compared with Buddha, Muhammad, Confucius, or anyone else. They are all dead. None of them made an atonement for sin. None of them bore the sins of the world before the judgment seat of God. If God sent his only Son into the world to bear every sin that I have ever committed, and he kills his Son in my place, and then says that if I put my trust in him, he is going to forgive every sin I have ever committed, and he's going to give me everlasting life so that I will never die, am I going to look at him and say "You have not done enough"?'

We are so arrogant that we demand God give us five doors into the sheepfold and we reject Jesus' own teaching about the broad way. 'For the gate is wide and the way is easy that leads to destruction, and those who enter by it are many' (Matt. 7:13). He continues, 'For the gate is narrow and the way is hard that leads to life, and those who find it are few' (Matt 7:14).

If you want to enter into the place of safety, you have to enter through Jesus. He promises that 'If anyone enters by me, he will be saved and will go in and out and find pasture. The thief comes only to steal and kill and destroy. I came that they may have life and have it abundantly' (John 10:9, 10). Jesus, by saying that he is the door to the sheepfold, is also saying he is the door to life itself – the transcendent kind of life that he came to give.

CHAPTER FOUR

The Good Shepherd

In the last chapter we looked at Jesus' pronouncement, 'I am the door,' in which he spoke of the door to the sheepfold – the gateway to eternal life in the Father's house. That saying was in response to the reaction against Jesus' healing of the man born blind. In the same passage Jesus calls himself 'the good shepherd' (John 10:11). I mentioned that we can distinguish between the sayings, 'I am the door to the sheepfold' and 'I am the good shepherd', but they belong together as part of the same saying. Before we study 'I am the good shepherd,' let me just make one last point about Jesus' statement, 'I am the door.' Remember at the end of that portion of his discussion the Lord said, 'If anyone enters by me, he will be saved' (verse 9). By doing this, Jesus directly connects salvation to his being the door.

After Paul gives his exposition of the gospel and the doctrine of justification by faith in Romans chapters 3 and 4, he outlines the benefits of our justification – what it is that

Christ has won for his people in his work of justification. He writes: 'Therefore, since we have been justified by faith, we have peace with God through our Lord Jesus Christ' (Rom. 5:1). That's the first benefit: we are reconciled to God. Our estrangement is over. There is no more warfare between God and us. We have peace because of our justification. The importance of having peace with the living God cannot be overstated. There is a reason why the common Hebrew greeting was and is 'Shalom', which literally means peace.

The second benefit the apostle mentions is that 'Through [Jesus] we have also obtained *access* by faith into this grace in which we stand' (verse 2, emphasis added). The word Paul uses to describe what Christ has won for us is *access* to the Father. That is what Jesus has in view when he refers to himself as the door. A door is a point of access. Jesus is that door, that way of access into the Father's presence. He is not just the proper and legitimate way in, but the only way in. Remember this word picture is tied to the whole idea of the imagery of the barrier to access that goes all the way back to the book of Genesis. When Adam and Eve were expelled from the garden of Eden, God posted an angel with a flaming sword at the gateway to paradise, prohibiting access back into the presence of God. We see that same imagery in the construction of the tabernacle and the temple in the Old Testament where there was a thick curtain that served as a line of separation that partitioned and screened the Holy of Holies from the Holy Place. Yet when Christ died, the veil of the temple was torn in two (from top to bottom, reminding us that it is God's work and not our own). The barrier was removed and access was now given to the people of God through the work of Christ. He is the door through the barrier. He is the door into the *inner sanctum*. He is the door by which we have access into God's presence.

The staff and rod of God

Keeping this in mind, let us go back to the passage and follow where Jesus adds to this imagery the idea of being the good shepherd:

> I am the good shepherd. The good shepherd lays down his life for the sheep. He who is a hired hand and not a shepherd, who does not own the sheep, sees the wolf coming and leaves the sheep and flees, and the wolf snatches them and scatters them. He flees because he is a hired hand and cares nothing for the sheep. I am the good shepherd. I know my own and my own know me (John 10:11-14).

Let's compare these words of Jesus with a very famous Psalm of David. In Psalm 23, David likens God to a shepherd,

> The LORD is my shepherd; I shall not want. He makes me lie down in green pastures. He leads me beside still waters. He restores my soul. He leads me in paths of righteousness for his name's sake. Even though I walk through the valley of the shadow of death, I will fear no evil (verses 1-4).

Why is evil not feared? Because the shepherd is guiding me. 'Your rod and your staff, they comfort me' (verse 4). This psalm contains interesting, vivid language because David is recalling his own days as a shepherd.

You remember when he was still a boy, and the troops of Israel were facing the armies of the Philistines, the giant Goliath came into the valley and called out a challenge for a champion to come forth from Israel who would take him on in hand-to-hand combat – winner takes all. Whoever wins the fight wins the day for his army. Remember how Saul looked around and could not find any of his warriors willing to go up against Goliath? David happens to appear because he's bringing his brothers a meal. He hears the challenge, the defiant words coming out of the mouth of this blasphemer Goliath, and David cannot believe that no one in Israel will stand up to him. So, he approaches Saul and says, 'I will go and fight the giant.' When they scoffed at him saying 'You're just a boy; you can't do this,' David said, 'I've handled a bear when it attacked my sheep. I've handled a lion when it attacked my sheep. God delivered me from both the bear and the lion. He'll deliver me from Goliath.' The rest is history.

David was experienced in fighting to defend his sheep. He had a rod and a staff. You've no doubt seen the shepherd's staff with the crook on the end. In his prayer, David says God's staff and rod gives him comfort. That crook that you see in pictures of the shepherd's staff, that bend on the end was for the shepherd to reach out and pull the sheep to safety if one veered toward the edge of a cliff or got caught in a ditch. The shepherd can rescue him because of his staff. The rod was the defensive club that the shepherd used to ward off the wild animals or even a thief attempting to steal the sheep. David looks to his God as the Great Shepherd, as if to say, 'O God, your staff and rod comfort me, because I know that your strength is there to protect me. And even if I go into the valley of the shadow of death, I don't have to go alone.'

We need to remember that God never promises his people that they will not enter the valley of the shadow of death. We all will enter into that vale at some point. The absolute promise God gives to his people is that he will never send us through it alone. I can't think of anywhere I would be frightened if I knew the Lord was with me. That is our hope as Christians – we can count upon the ultimate Shepherd of our souls to be with us, no matter what. What a wonderful thing David, the shepherd king of Israel, anticipates in the coming of his greater Son, in the incarnation of the divine Shepherd, the one who is celebrated in Psalm 23, the one who indeed is 'the Good Shepherd'!

The good shepherd lays down his life

Jesus says, 'I am the good shepherd. The good shepherd gives his life for his sheep' (John 10:11). Notice the first thing he does here is to contrast the good shepherd from the hired hand. The difference is plain. The good shepherd owns the sheep; the sheep are his. He makes his own personal livelihood from the sheep, so he is committed to their welfare. The hired hand is someone brought in for an hourly rate, hired temporarily to look after the sheep, but he has no vested interest in the flock. He doesn't own the sheep and has no affection for them. He has no ultimate concern for their well-being; so when the devouring animal or thief comes, the hired hand runs from the danger.

Jesus is saying, 'That is not how I am with my sheep, because I am the good shepherd, and the good shepherd defends his sheep to the death.' Jesus says here, anticipating the cross, 'I lay down my life for my sheep.' This isn't the first or only time that Jesus uses that language in the New Testament. Elsewhere, he makes it clear that when he as the good shepherd gives his life for his sheep, his life isn't being taken from him. Do you remember how he's taunted when he's on the cross? 'You saved others, but you cannot save yourself. Come down off the cross.' Jesus knew he had legions of angels at his disposal and he could have called upon heaven to remove him from the cross, but if he had done that he wouldn't have accomplished what he came to do. In like manner, on the occasion when they sent out guards to arrest him and it wasn't his time, he walked right through them. Not a single guard laid a hand on him because he had authority to lay down his life and authority to take it back up again. He didn't die until it was time to die. He even told his captors, 'You would have no authority over me at all unless it had been given you from above' (John 19:11). In those words Jesus makes it clear that even his death is a voluntary sacrifice. He lays down his own life, not for his own benefit but for his sheep. His sheep are the ones whom God the Father has given to him. He said, 'My sheep hear my voice, and I know them, and they follow me' (10:27).

One flock, one shepherd

Jesus solidifies this concept in saying:

> He who is a hired hand and not a shepherd, who does not own the sheep, sees the wolf coming and leaves the sheep and flees, and the wolf snatches them and scatters them. He flees because he is a hired hand and cares nothing for the sheep. I am the good shepherd. I know my own and my own know me, just as the Father knows me and I know the Father; and I lay down my life for the sheep. And I have other sheep that are not of this fold. I must bring them also, and they will listen to my voice. So there will be one flock, one shepherd (verses 12-16).

With this, Jesus introduced into the lesson something that was totally inflammatory to the Pharisees who were listening. Here, Jesus compares the relationship between the good shepherd and the sheep – how the shepherd knows the sheep and loves the sheep, and the sheep likewise know the shepherd and love the shepherd – to his relationship with the Father. The Father knows the good shepherd, just like the good shepherd knows his sheep, and he knows the Father.

Jesus also makes the somewhat cryptic comment, 'And I have other sheep that are not of this fold.' Remember when we looked at the 'I am the door' statement, that the sheepfold would contain more than one flock from more than one shepherd. It was only because the shepherds knew their sheep that they didn't get mixed up and lost in the large mass of sheep. But Jesus adds, 'I have other sheep that are not of this fold.' I've seen many interpretations of this passage, some of them even bizarre, but I think it's pretty easy to discern what Jesus is speaking about considering his Jewish audience. He's speaking of the mystery of the new covenant, that God's sheep are not limited to Israel but are from every tongue, tribe and nation. He's bringing sheep from the Gentiles into his body, the church. In his church there is one flock and one Shepherd, not a different shepherd for the Gentiles and one for the Jews. There is one flock and one Shepherd and all his people belong to him.

I once heard a radio broadcast by Dr James Montgomery Boice in which he was talking about the propensity we have as Christians to think the only way with which God is pleased is our own way. If someone is doing the work of the kingdom differently from the way we would do it, then he's probably not even in the kingdom in the first place. The truth is that no one has a perfect grasp or understanding of the things of God. When we see someone who's in a different church or a different ministry from our own – doing things a little differently from how we would do it, but nonetheless doing the work of Christ – we're supposed to rejoice. Even as zealous as we are for what we believe is the truth, we still have to recognize that among real Christians there are all kinds of different styles, systems, ministries and concerns. They don't always perfectly match up but we're all in Christ. We're all part of the same flock and we look to the Good Shepherd, who gives us our marching orders.

Jesus says, 'For this reason the Father loves me, because I lay down my life that I may take it up again. No one takes it from me, but I lay it down of my own accord. I have authority to lay it down, and I have authority to take it up again' (verses 17, 18). Again, he refers to the temple he's going to rebuild in three days after it has been destroyed. I wonder, who might have understood these words at the moment they were spoken? And who among those there would not think of those things on Resurrection Sunday? 'I have authority to lay it down, and I have authority to take it up again. This charge I have received from my Father' (verse 18). We are told elsewhere that Jesus is the Bishop and the Shepherd of our souls. That's the vocation God has given to Christ. He is the Son of God and, as the Son of God, God makes him responsible for, and gives him authority over, our very souls. He is the Good Shepherd of our souls.

Before Jesus left, in one of his last discussions with his disciples after the resurrection, he asked Peter three times, 'Simon, son of John, do you love me more than these?' And three times Peter replied, 'Yes Lord; you know that I love you' (John 21:15). Three times Jesus said to Peter (and by extension the church of all ages), 'If you love me, feed my sheep.'

They're not Peter's sheep. They're not my sheep. They're his sheep, and we are called to follow in the footsteps of the one who is the Good Shepherd.

CHAPTER FIVE

The Resurrection and the Life

I n this chapter, we're going to look at the important declaration Jesus made when he visited Mary and Martha at Bethany after the death of Lazarus. In response to Lazarus' death, Jesus said, 'I am the resurrection and the life' (John 11:25). To set the context for this statement, let's further consider John 11, where the author begins by telling us that Lazarus had become ill and so his sisters sent a message to Jesus imploring him to come and help, saying, 'Lord, he whom you love is ill' (verse 3). When Jesus heard this, He responded, 'This illness does not lead to death. It is for the glory of God, so that the Son of God may be glorified through it' (verse 4). That, of course, was an encouraging response. Then however we are told, 'Now Jesus loved Martha and her sister and Lazarus. So, when he heard that Lazarus was ill, he stayed two days longer in the place where he was' (verses 5, 6).

This is a jolting statement. We would think, as the sisters of Lazarus likely did, that Jesus would have come immediately. Instead, he stayed where he was two additional days:

> Then after this he said to the disciples, 'Let us go to Judea again.' The disciples said to him, 'Rabbi, the Jews were just now seeking to stone you, and are you going there again?' Jesus answered, 'Are there not twelve hours in the day? If anyone walks in the day, he does not stumble, because he sees the light of this world. But if anyone walks in the night, he stumbles, because the light is not in him.' After saying these things, he said to them, 'Our friend Lazarus has fallen asleep, but I go to awaken him.' The disciples said to him, 'Lord, if he has fallen asleep, he will recover.' Now Jesus had spoken of his death, but they thought that he meant taking rest in sleep. Then Jesus told them plainly, 'Lazarus has died, and for your sake I am glad that I was not there, so that you may believe. But let us go to him' (verses 7-15).

This is cryptic language Jesus uses with his disciples. Why was he glad his disciples were not there? Is he simply suggesting that he was glad that they weren't there because they wouldn't have to witness the demise of Lazarus, or is he saying, 'You haven't begun to see what I'm going to make manifest in the light'? Either way, Jesus says, 'Let us go to him.'

John goes on to record, 'So Thomas, called the Twin, said to his fellow disciples, "Let us also go, that we may die with him"' (verse 16). Jesus' disciples assumed that if Jesus returned to Judea, this so close to Jerusalem and to the seat of the authority of those who were in opposition to him, that they were risking their lives. That's why the disciples didn't want Jesus to go. When Jesus said he was going to Lazarus, Thomas prompted the disciples to follow, believing that if Jesus were to die, they would be able to die beside him. Of course, Thomas' attitude and understanding would change dramatically in just a few short days.

The definitional reality of the resurrection

Let's consider the record of what takes place when Jesus comes to the home of Lazarus. 'Now, when Jesus came, he found that Lazarus had already been in the tomb four days' (verse 17). This minor detail in the narrative was significant to the ancient Jews. Most Semitic people of that day held the belief that when a person died, the soul that had departed from the body would come back and visit the body periodically for a few days after death. By the fourth day, however, when it was obvious that decay had begun to set in, it was believed that the soul had abandoned the body once and for all. It's not as though they believed you weren't really dead unless you were dead for four days, but that it was now impossible for any kind of revival to take place. John gives us this detail so we know the bodily corruption had begun to set in.

'Bethany was near Jerusalem, about two miles off' (verse 18). If you've ever been to Jerusalem, you know that between Jerusalem and the Mount of Olives there is a deep valley —

the Kidron Valley – and on the slope opposite the Mount of Olives is the town of Bethany. From Bethany you can look right across the ravine into the old city of Jerusalem. It was a short distance that could be walked easily. We read, 'Many of the Jews had come to Martha and Mary to console them concerning their brother' (verse 19). We see that a multitude of Jewish people had made the trip up the Mount of Olives to Bethany, to the home of Mary and Martha.

'So when Martha heard that Jesus was coming, she went and met him, but Mary remained seated in the house. Martha said to Jesus, "Lord, if you had been here, my brother would not have died"' (verse 20). Martha, who was desperate for Jesus to come to rescue her brother from his illness, was not only upset by the death of her brother but also upset by what she considered a failure on Jesus' part to do what she had expected. So she met Jesus with a rebuke, saying, 'Lord, if you had been here, my brother would not have died. But even now I know that whatever you ask from God, God will give you' (verses 21, 22). On the one hand she rebukes him, and on the other she says, in effect, 'I know that whatever God wants, we're willing to accept. And whatever you ask of God, God will give you.' In response Jesus said to her, 'Your brother will rise again' (verse 23).

We don't have any reason to believe Martha was expecting Jesus to resurrect Lazarus. The reason I don't think that she was expecting Jesus to raise her brother from the dead is because she then said, 'I know that he will rise again in the resurrection on the last day' (verse 24). In other words, she was saying, 'Yes, Lord, I believe in the future resurrection, and I know at some point my brother will rise again.' Now remember, not everyone in Israel believed in the future resurrection. Among the leaders of the Jewish people the Pharisees did, but the Sadducees didn't. Martha believed, like the Pharisees, in the future resurrection.

It is at this moment that Jesus pronounces the 'I am.' Jesus does not say, 'I will be the one who will raise Lazarus in the last day.' Instead he says, 'I am the resurrection and the life' (verse 25). This is an astonishing claim and declaration, joining the other 'I am' sayings we've already examined.

Jesus not only gives light to the world, but he is the light of the world. Jesus not only helps people through the door to everlasting life, but he himself is the door. This was commonplace for idiomatic expressions of the people in that day. If something was closely associated with a particular person, that person would be identified by it as a manner of speaking. We learn, for example, in John's first epistle that 'God is love' (1 John 4:8). What he is saying, idiomatically, is that God is so closely connected with love that it could be said that he is the definitional reality of love. Likewise, Jesus is so connected with power over death and eternal life, the power of the resurrection, that he is saying, 'Not only do I have the power to raise people from the dead, and not only do I have the power to raise myself from the dead, but *I am* the resurrection.'

Hope of the resurrection

In the Old Testament Job raised the question: 'If a man dies, shall he live again?' (Job 14:14). This question has been on the minds of every human being since death was first experienced. In every culture, in every tribe and every civilization we see people speculating about the question of death and the afterlife. The obvious question is 'When I die, is that the end? Is the whole of my existence summed up between the two points of birth and death – or is there something more?' Life is so precious that there beats within every human heart a hope that there will be victory over the grave. Look at the writings of the philosopher Plato who, in his discussions concerning the death of Socrates, gives a philosophical argument for life after death. He makes an argument from analogy, which is borrowed from the cyclical character of life and death in the realm of nature: for grass to grow, seed must be planted and the seed has to die, but when the seed dies and the shell rots, then the seed germinates and new life emerges. We see these analogies of life-from-death in nature and we also see in nature something that the apostle Paul pointed out; there are different kinds of life on earth.

If you've studied biology and zoology, you see countless living things inhabiting this planet. The question is always raised: is *thanatos* – is 'death' – the end of every form of life as we know it? Or, is there something afterwards, as in nature when one thing dies and changes its form to come back through metamorphosis into another way of being?

The ancient Pythagoreans had a view of reincarnation, which they called the transmigration of the soul, where the soul experiences repeated incarnations. At the end of the day, all of this – the views of Plato and the Pythagoreans – are speculative. The greatest hope we have in the world for life after death is found in the historical resurrection of Christ, which the New Testament sets before us, not as an isolated incident, but as an event that is the first of a multitude of similar events to follow. Jesus is raised from the dead for us, so that we will also participate in that resurrection. That is at the core of the hope of the Christian faith.

We know that one of the reasons the first-century Christians were willing to undergo martyrdom was because they were convinced of the resurrection. They were convinced that death did not have the final word. They believed that death, far from being Satan's victory over us, had instead been defeated. For believers in Christ, death is not the end of life but simply a transition from our current earthly existence into eternal life. All of that comes down, not to an argument, but to a *person*. When Jesus says, thinking about the future resurrection, 'I am the resurrection and the life,' he had already taught about his being the author of life; that he came to make life – spiritual life, eternal life – a reality for his people. 'I came that [you] might have life, and have it abundantly' (John 10:10).

Life everlasting

Jesus expands on this by saying, 'I am the resurrection and the life. Whoever believes in me, though he die, yet shall he live, and everyone who lives and believes in me shall never die. Do you believe this?' (11:25, 26). This sounds, at first glance, somewhat contradictory because he says that if you believe in him, even if you die, you're going to live. But then he says if you believe in him, you will never die. However, what Jesus is saying is that those who are in him – in faith – never die, in one sense. In another sense they still die, yet continue to live. The idea here is that *zōē* – this eternal life that he comes to give to his people – begins in the soul the moment faith is born in the heart. *Zōē* cannot be killed by *thanatos*. Physical death cannot destroy the life that Christ puts into the believer. Even when we experience physical death, we don't die.

Behind the concept of resurrection is Christ's promise of the continuity of personal existence. The day that your body dies is not the day that you die. That is the day you become more conscious of reality than you have ever been. In a very real sense, the ultimate life for which God has made us as living beings doesn't begin until we cross the veil. That is why the apostle Paul can say he was torn between two alternatives. He expresses his dilemma in these words: 'My desire is to depart and be with Christ, for that is far better' (Phil. 1:23). On the one hand, Paul communicates this deep desire to leave; yet he also has a desire to stay and serve the church, which is more needful. His work wasn't done, but he was eager to see Jesus and to be with him. Paul's hope was founded on Jesus' promise. Jesus, as he approached his own death, told his disciples, 'In my Father's house are many rooms. If it were not so, would I have told you that I go to prepare a place for you?' (John 14:2).

As he is comforting Martha, Jesus tells her, 'Look Martha, we're not only talking future resurrection; you are talking to the one who is the resurrection and the life.' And he asks, 'Do you believe this?' She said to him, 'Yes, Lord; I believe that you are the Christ, the Son of God, who is coming into the world.' When she had said this, she went and called her sister Mary, saying in private, 'The Teacher is here and is calling for you' (11:26-28). What follows is Mary's echoing the lament Martha made in verse 21: 'Lord, if you had been here, my brother would not have died' (verse 32).

It is here that we see Jesus fulfil what he is claiming about himself – that he *is* the resurrection:

When Jesus saw her weeping, and the Jews who had come with her also weeping, he was deeply moved in his spirit and greatly troubled. And he said, 'Where have you laid him?' They said to him, 'Lord, come and see.' Jesus wept. So the Jews said, 'See how he loved him!' But some of them said, 'Could not he who opened the eyes of the blind man also have kept this man from dying?' Then Jesus, deeply moved again, came to the tomb. It was a cave, and a stone lay against it. Jesus said, 'Take away the stone.' Martha, the sister of the dead man, said to him, 'Lord, by this time there will be an odour, for he has been dead four days.' Jesus said to her, 'Did I not tell you that if you believed you would see the glory of God?' So they took away the stone. And Jesus lifted up his eyes and said, 'Father, I thank you that you have heard me. I knew that you always hear me, but I said this on account of the people standing around, that they may believe that you sent me.' When he had said these things, he cried out with a loud voice, 'Lazarus, come out' (verses 33-43).

When Jesus stood in front of this open tomb with the corpse of Lazarus inside, he didn't whisper in a meek voice, instead he *shouted* into the tomb, 'Lazarus, come out!' I think it's important that we pause for a moment to remember this is how God Almighty created the universe. He created the world out of nothing by the sheer power of his divine call. He created all that there is by his word and so also by his Word – Jesus Christ – Lazarus' corpse is empowered to come back to life. As soon as Jesus cries in that loud voice and gives the imperative of God himself to the dead Lazarus, his heart began to beat and to pump blood through his vessels. Brain activity was reignited. The rotting tissue was healed. Strength entered back into his bones and Lazarus, who had died, came out, bound hand and foot with long strips of cloth – yet he was alive. Jesus said to those there, 'Unbind him, and let him go' (verse 44).

Wouldn't you have loved to see that, the power of Christ in the presence of death? Christ later identifies himself in this way when he appeared to John on the island of Patmos in the first chapter of the book of Revelation. When John sees him, he tells us that he fell at Christ's feet as though dead. But Jesus laid his hands on him and said, 'Fear not, I am the first and the last, and the living one. I died, and behold I am alive forevermore, and I have the keys of Death and Hades' (Rev. 1:17, 18). The one who is the resurrection and the life has the key to unlock the grave and overcome the power of death so that we have nothing to fear. For the Christian, the resurrection is a magnificent entrance to the supreme setting of human life. It's at the heart of the Christian faith. Without it, Christianity is simply empty, irrelevant and vainly moralistic in the eyes of the modern person. As long as there's life and as long as there is death, there is no one more relevant than Jesus Christ, the Resurrection and the Life.

CHAPTER SIX

The Way, the Truth and the Life

As we continue to look at the 'I am' sayings of Jesus, the one we're going to focus in on in this chapter has multiple attributes associated with it. It appears in one of the most popular chapters in all of sacred Scripture, chapter 14 of the Gospel of John. The beginning of chapter 14 is familiar to most of us, and gives the context in which this 'I am' saying appears. It begins with the Upper Room Discourse that Jesus has with his disciples on the night in which he was betrayed, arrested and sent to trial.

Jesus, meeting with his disciples, says to them:

Let not your hearts be troubled. Believe in God; believe also in me. In my Father's house are many rooms. If it were not so, would I have told you that I go to prepare a place for you? And if I go and prepare a place for you, I will come again and will take you to myself, that where I am you may be also. And you know the way to where I am going (John 14:1-4).

This is the context for this 'I am' saying of Jesus. Jesus is preparing his disciples for his death and telling them he will be going away soon. They should have known where he was going for he had already told them that he was going to prepare a place for them in his Father's house.

Knowing the way

Thomas, confused and bewildered by these statements, says to Jesus, 'Lord, we do not know where you are going. How can we know the way?' (verse 5). The concept of 'the way' was important in the early church. We have already looked at it briefly in terms of Jesus' statement, 'I am the door,' which is the means by which access is gained into the kingdom. In the early church we know believers in Christ were not first called 'Christians.' The term *Christian* was originally a pejorative term, an insult that the enemies of the followers of Christ used against them. They were first called Christians in Antioch, but before this they were called 'the People of the Way,' because Jesus had spoken about his being the way to God, the way to the kingdom and the way to the Father. So, Thomas asks, 'How can we know the way? Give us a map. Give us the directions. How are we going to know how to get there?' It's in this context that Jesus answers Thomas' question with these words, 'I am the way, and the truth, and the life' (verse 6).

The exclusiveness of Christ as the way is contained in his statement, 'No one comes to the Father except through me' (verse 7). Jesus declared the same thing when he said that he was the door through which men must enter into the kingdom. And here he now says with absolute clarity that 'No one comes to the Father except through me.' The statement can sound jolting to our ears because it's on a collision course with Western pluralism. The church is increasingly captured by an all-inclusive theology where every world religion is equally valid and true, widening the gap from the exclusiveness that Jesus articulates on the night before he died. The culture says there are many roads to heaven, that heaven is at the top of the mountain and there are many different paths to reach the peak. Jesus says, however, that there's only one road and he *is* that road. That's what the word *way* means in the text, 'the road, the pathway that one must follow to get to a desired destination.' He is not *a* road, *a* way, but *the* road, *the* way.

This is how he answers Thomas initially, 'If you had known me, you would have known my Father also. From now on you do know him and have seen him' (verse 7). That's one of the most radical statements Jesus ever made – from now on they can say that they've seen the Father.

Philip responds, saying to him, 'Lord, show us the Father, and it is enough for us' (verse 8). It's as if what Philip is saying, 'We've been with you now these three years and we can't believe what our eyes have beheld. We've seen you raise people from the dead. We've seen you give sight to the blind. We've seen you give hearing to the deaf. We've seen you walk on the water, and some of us have even seen you transfigured before our very eyes. We have seen amazing things, but we're still not satisfied. We want the big one. We want the one that even Moses was denied, and of which every person has been denied since Adam and Eve were banished from Paradise. We want to see God. Not only would seeing him help us in our quest to grow in obedience, but it would satisfy our souls.' The disciples had said several times, 'Just do this one last thing and we'll never ask again.' We know people like that. How many times have we said that to God? 'God, just answer this one prayer, and I'll never ask for another thing.' And when God answers it, the next day we ask, 'Just one more.' We never stop. Likewise, here's Philip, saying, 'Show us the Father, and that's enough.'

If there's any place in Scripture where we see Jesus almost becoming impatient, annoyed and irritated with his disciples, I think maybe this is the place. We operate at a disadvantage when we read these words because they don't communicate the non-verbal gestures and vocal inflection that accompanied them. Just by changing the tone of our voice or raising our eyebrows, we can take a simple statement and make it satirical. We learn those subtle cues of communication, but they are not always revealed to us in Scripture. Yet Jesus seems to be exasperated here when he says, 'Have I been with you so long, and you still do not know me, Philip?' (verse 9). I think that communicates a serious rebuke.

Then comes the dramatic addition, continued in verse 9: 'Whoever has seen me has seen the Father. How can you say, "Show us the Father?"' Jesus is saying in effect 'What do you think I've been doing all this time? You're talking to God incarnate. You're talking to the express image of his person. You're talking to the visible manifestation of the invisible God.'

This is one of the most extraordinary claims Jesus made. It never ceases to amaze me when people declare that Jesus never makes any claim to deity in the New Testament. Such people are being intellectually dishonest. Jesus clearly makes such a claim here as well as in other places. If you've seen Jesus, you've seen the Father:

> Do you not believe that I am in the Father and the Father is in me? The words that I say to you I do not speak on my own authority, but the Father who dwells in me does his works. Believe me that I am in the Father and the Father is in me, or else believe on account of the works themselves (verses 10, 11).

There is such a unity here in the Godhead between the Father and the Son that, if you see the Son, you see the Father. If you know the Son, you know the Father. This was the point of dispute Jesus had with the Pharisees, who claimed to be disciples of God the Father but who rejected Jesus.

Jesus, the truth

Let's come back to the multiple statements Jesus makes in 'I am the way, the truth, and the life.' I believe that this statement, 'I am … the truth,' is one of the most important of the 'I am' sayings. In it, Jesus identifies himself with truth.

In the early 1970s, Ligonier Ministries put on a seminar in Western Pennsylvania on the question of the inerrancy of sacred Scripture. We had scholars from around the world come in and present papers. With no collusion or pre-planning, every one of us based our defence of the authority of the Bible on the authority of Jesus by showing that he believed Scripture to be God's true, unbreakable word. When I was studying higher critical theories, it was even commonplace among critical scholars to acknowledge that Jesus embraced the first-century Jewish view of the Scripture – that it was the inspired word of God. They went on to say however that Jesus, in his human nature, was not omniscient, he did not know everything, and was unaware that the Bible was not inspired. Those scholars believe Jesus made a mistake common in his day when he said, 'Moses wrote of me,' because he didn't realize that Moses didn't write the Pentateuch. They believe Jesus was simply wrong in his earthly assessments about how the Scripture had come to be. However, the higher critics are right that his human nature was not omniscient. They're quite right that, in his human nature, there were things Jesus didn't know. The divine nature was omniscient, but his human nature wasn't. Since the human nature was not omniscient, the critics reasoned, it was perfectly alright that there were things Jesus didn't know.

Jesus, our Lord and Saviour, was ignorant about certain things. He had a duty not to claim knowledge he didn't have, yet he taught the people of God with absolute authority. He told God's people certain things about sacred Scripture, and he taught them – according to the critics – erroneously. Ignorance would not excuse that because, if I don't know something, I'm supposed to know that I don't know it. I'm supposed to bracket my claims of expertise in light of the limits of my knowledge. For Jesus, there were no brackets. He said, 'I am the truth.' Thus he identified himself with truth. And when he was on trial before Pontius Pilate, Pilate asked him if he was a king and Jesus said, 'For this purpose I was born and for this purpose I have come into the world – to bear witness to the truth' (John 18:37).

We live in an age when truth has been despised and lies slain in the street. People in the church claim it's not doctrine that matters but relationships. Truth is not seen as important – except of course that when we say what's important, we're saying this is an important truth! However, we have no way to evaluate the axiom unless we first have an understanding of truth. It is the truth of God that is supposed to define how we are to relate to one another. To set relationships and truth against each other, therefore, is to divide and to tear apart what God has joined. Truth and relationships are to be held together and are equally sacred to the people of God. How can we despise truth without despising Christ at the same time? He is the truth. I take great comfort in that knowledge because virtually every principle the Bible teaches is denied somewhere in our culture. How do you know what's true? We go to the source. We are to go to the source of truth, and to the one who *is* the source of truth. The embodiment of truth is Christ. He is the incarnation of truth itself.

In his saying, 'I am … the life,' Jesus is once again introducing the principle we saw when studying 'I am the resurrection' and 'I am the good shepherd.' Life itself would be impossible apart from Christ – any life, not just spiritual life. Apart from him, there is no life at all. Jesus is saying to his disciples, to Thomas and Philip, who are befuddled at this difficult time after the Lord's Supper, 'I am the way, the truth, and the life.' All three of these things find their essence, and subsistence in Christ.

CHAPTER SEVEN

The True Vine

It is important to remember that the 'I am' sayings we have examined are all prefaced by the unusual Greek construction *egō eimi*, which is the same combination of words used in the Greek translation of the Old Testament for God's sacred name, Yahweh – 'I AM WHO I AM' (Exod. 3:14). We now come to chapter 15 of John's Gospel where we have the seventh 'I am' saying in which Jesus says:

> I am the true vine, and my Father is the vinedresser. Every branch in me that does not bear fruit he takes away, and every branch that does bear fruit he prunes, that it may bear more fruit. Already you are clean because of the word that I have spoken to you. Abide in me, and I in you. As the branch cannot bear fruit by itself, unless it abides in the vine, neither can you, unless you abide in me. I am the vine; you are the branches. Whoever abides in me and I in him, he it is that bears much fruit, for apart from me you can do nothing (John 15:1-5).

Notice in verse 5 he says, 'I am the vine; you are the branches.' This is slightly different from what he says in the first verse where he calls himself not merely the vine but 'the *true* vine' (emphasis added). So, we have two things happening in this 'I am' saying that are important. The first part of the text, which is often overlooked, is the first important statement Jesus makes when he says, 'I am the true vine.'

Usually when somebody makes a statement like that, it's intended to stand in stark contrast to something else. Jesus could have simply said, and indeed later does, 'I am the vine.' By adding the word 'true,' he is implying that there exists another vine that is false. In this case, there was in fact a false vine. Clearly, the hearers of Jesus would recognize the allusion he was making when he calls himself the true vine. The metaphor of the vine was not something new to the ears of the Jewish people. It was an important metaphor used in the Old Testament regularly to describe the relationship between God and Israel – between God and his people – in which God was the vinedresser and Israel was the vine.

The corrupt vine

To properly grasp this concept let's take a look at some of the Old Testament references to this relationship between God and Israel. First of all, Psalm 80 begins with these words, 'Give ear, O Shepherd of Israel' (verse 1). Isn't it interesting that the psalmist refers to God here as the Shepherd, just as

Jesus had called himself the good shepherd? The psalmist continues:

> You who lead Joseph like a flock. You who are enthroned upon the cherubim [a reference to the ark of the covenant which was adorned with the figures of the cherubim on either side] shine forth. Before Ephraim and Benjamin and Manasseh, stir up your might and come to save us! Restore us, O God; let your face shine, that we may be saved! O LORD God of hosts, how long will you be angry with your people's prayers? You have fed them with the bread of tears and given them tears to drink in full measure. You make us an object of contention for our neighbours and our enemies laugh among themselves (verses 1-6).

The psalmist at this point is expressing a lament. He is weeping before God because Israel is experiencing God's anger and judgment. Continuing on, the psalmist takes up the image we're interested in by saying:

> You brought a vine out of Egypt; you drove out the nations and planted it. You cleared the ground for it; it took deep root and filled the land. The mountains were covered with its shade, the mighty cedars with its branches. It sent out its branches to the sea and its shoots to the River (verses 8-11).

Do you see how this imagery refers back to the Exodus? God brought his people, a vine, out of Egypt and prepared a place for it – the Promised Land – with enough room for the vine to be planted deeply and spread out through the

Holy Land. You get the sense of the tender care of the vineyard owner and the intentionality of his endeavour. It is here that we see the fruitfulness God bestowed on his vine. He nurtured it and it thrived, spreading across the land.

The psalmist continues his plea:

> Turn again, O God of hosts! Look down from heaven, and see; have regard for this vine, the stock that your right hand planted, and for the son whom you made strong for yourself. They have burned it with fire; they have cut it down; may they perish at the rebuke of your face! But let your hand be on the man of your right hand, the son of man whom you have made strong for yourself! Then we shall not turn back from you; give us life, and we will call upon your name! Restore us, O LORD God of hosts! Let your face shine, that we may be saved! (verses 14-19).

The phrase 'But let your hand be on the man of your right hand, the son of man whom you have made strong for yourself' (verse 17), could simply refer to the nation Israel, to David, or to the Messiah who appears later in history under the title of the Son of Man. Whatever the case, the plea in this prayer is for God to return to the vineyard and save that which he had planted.

We see a similar song in celebration – or lament – in chapter 5 of the book of the prophet Isaiah:

> Let me sing for my beloved my love song concerning his vineyard; my beloved had a vineyard on a very fertile hill. He dug it and cleared it of stones, and planted it with choice

vines; he built a watchtower in the midst of it, and hewed out a wine vat in it; and he looked for it to yield grapes, but it yielded wild grapes. And now, O inhabitants of Jerusalem and men of Judah, judge between me and my vineyard. What more was there to do for my vineyard, that I have not done in it? When I looked for it to yield grapes, why did it yield wild grapes? And now I will tell you what I will do to my vineyard. I will remove its hedge, and it shall be devoured; I will break down its wall, and it shall be trampled down. I will make it a waste; it shall not be pruned or hoed, and briers and thorns shall grow up; I will also command the clouds that they rain no rain upon it. For the vineyard of the LORD of hosts is the house of Israel, and the men of Judah are his pleasant planting; and he looked for justice, but behold, bloodshed; for righteousness, but behold, an outcry! (verses 1-7).

We see both in Psalm 80 and in this passage in the prophet Isaiah that God expresses his wrath against Israel, the nation he brought out of bondage, planted, nurtured, watered and grew. When he expected fruit from it, he only got wild grapes. Israel became the corrupt vine and so Jesus came and said to the people, 'I am the true vine and my Father is the vinedresser.'

The true vine

What is radical about this is that Jesus is saying he is the embodiment of Israel. You see this frequently hinted at in the New Testament in allusions to Old Testament events, which are then applied to Jesus. Remember that when Jesus was born and Herod sought to take his life, Joseph was warned in a dream, and so he took Mary and the baby, and fled to Egypt. Then after Herod died and it was safe, Joseph was told to bring the child back from Egypt into the Promised Land in order 'to fulfil what the Lord had spoken by Hosea the prophet, "Out of Egypt I called my Son"' (Matt. 2:15, citing Hos. 11:1). In a somewhat cryptic reference, Christ becomes the embodiment and the incarnation of all that takes place in the Old Testament with respect to the nation of Israel. He is so representative of his people as the Messiah that he, in a real sense, is Israel. In the same way, John introduces his Gospel with respect to Jesus being the *Logos* – 'the Word of God' in flesh – saying, 'And the Word became flesh and *dwelt* among us' (John 1:14, emphasis added). This word 'dwelt' in the text is the Greek verb *skēnoō*, which means 'to pitch a tent' or 'to tabernacle.' Thus John is saying that, 'Jesus pitched his tent; he pitched his tabernacle with us.' In doing this, John shows that the whole tabernacle experience of the Old Testament points away from itself toward the one who would come and embody everything symbolized in the tent of meeting; that would be God with us, Immanuel.

Fruitfulness of the branches

Jesus begins his discourse by saying to his hearers, 'Every branch in me that does not bear fruit [the Father] takes away, and every branch that does bear fruit he prunes, that it may bear more fruit' (John 15:2). To have the optimum production of fruit from a vineyard it's vital that the vines be pruned on a regular basis, even the branches that are fruit-bearing. The branches bearing fruit need to be pruned back to increase their productivity. But every vine will have branches that die and the vinedresser comes and cuts off those dead branches. What are they used for? These dead pieces of wood have an ignoble end. You don't take them to the carpenter's shop and give them to a cabinetmaker – they're worthless. The only purpose they can serve is building a fire. And so, the dead branches are removed from the vine and burned.

Jesus is making an illustration here of the church. Remember he says that the church is made up of the sheep and the goats. It's made up of the tares and the wheat. There are always, in every church, people who make an outward profession of faith, but their profession is not true. They're invaders into the body of Christ. They are tares that grow among the wheat. It's up to the Lord who tends to his field to come and root out the tares. The warning here is that there will be unbelieving people in the church with true Christians, but they're fruitless. They make a profession of faith, but they're like clouds that are empty of water. They have the outer appearance of faith, but they don't bear any fruit. We're not describing Christians here who don't bear fruit, because there's no such thing as a Christian who doesn't bear fruit. If you don't bear fruit, that's a clear indication you're not a believer. You're merely dead wood trying to attach yourself to the true vine. That's not going to work; God is going to cut you off, just as he did to the nation of Israel. He took the dead wood of Israel, cut it off, and threw it into the fire.

There's a play on words here in the Greek, however, that doesn't translate well into English, where Jesus says he prunes the branch that it may bear more fruit. He says to his disciples, 'Already you are clean because of the word that I have spoken to you' (verse 3). There's a word for 'taking away' and then there's a word for 'adding' – the idea of cleansing and pruning – *katharos*, from which we get the word *catharsis*. Jesus is saying to his disciples, 'I've already made you clean.' His true disciples had already been cleansed because of all he had spoken to them. He says then, 'Abide in me, and I in you. As the branch cannot bear fruit by itself, unless it abides in the vine, neither can you, unless you abide in me' (verse 4). If there are no branches on the vine, there can be no fruit from the vine. The branch has to be connected to the vine for the fruit to grow and be useful. So, Jesus is saying, 'I'm the vine. You have to abide in me. I have to abide in you. You have to stay close to me if you want to be productive as a Christian. You've already been cleansed. You're already in me, and I am in you.' The degree of your fruitfulness as a Christian will be directly proportionate to how close you stay to Christ, how much you feed on his word, and how intimate your relationship is to him. If you're barely attached, your fruit will be barely productive.

I sometimes hear a disparaging of good works among Protestants. Since we have fought the battle of the Reformation – remembering that our salvation is not based upon our works but on the works of Christ and that we're saved by faith alone – some believe once they are in Christ it doesn't matter whether they are productive or not. Our good works don't save us, but we *are* saved to do good works. The work of Christ is not simply to forgive us of sin, but to remake us into the image of the Son. If we study the teaching of Jesus in the New Testament, he is constantly calling his people to bear fruit, to make manifest the faith they have through their works. The Christian stays close to Christ and receives nurture from him, and through his loving discipline, the Christian yields the fruit of the kingdom. In the New Testament church, God doesn't want wild grapes, he wants fruit.

CHAPTER EIGHT

Before Abraham Was, I Am

When we normally talk about the 'I am' sayings of Jesus in the church, they are listed as including seven pronouncements, which have already been considered in this book. This chapter represents the eighth 'I am' saying which many commentators add to the list, even though this pronouncement differs structurally from the others. Each of the other 'I am' sayings begin with the words *egō eimi* – 'I am the vine,' 'I am the good shepherd,' 'I am the door,' and so on. In this case, the pronouncement ends with these words. And I believe that this saying is, in fact, the most dramatic of all: 'Jesus said to [the Pharisees], "Truly, truly, I say to you, before Abraham was, I am"' (John 8:58).

To catch the weight of this pronouncement, we have to begin much earlier in the eighth chapter of John's Gospel to see what provoked this discussion about Christ's relationship to Abraham: 'So Jesus said to the Jews who had believed him, "If you abide in my word, you are truly my disciples, and you will know the truth, and the truth will set you free"' (verses 31, 32). This is one of the most important statements Jesus ever uttered. The word 'if' that Jesus uses is an important, necessary condition. He says, 'If you abide in my word, you are truly my disciples' (verse 31). A true disciple is not one who gives attention to the words of Christ in a casual manner. A true disciple of Christ abides and maintains his posture of learning at the feet of Jesus. He then continues the saying, 'and you will know the truth, and the truth will set you free' (verse 32). In these words Jesus speaks of the liberation God brings to those who ingest, as it were, the truth that he reveals. This promise is given to those who believe Jesus, to his true disciples.

For those who did not believe in Jesus, these words were provocative. The people became enraged. 'They answered him, "Abraham is our father"' (verse 39). They challenged Jesus' words, claiming to follow after God as Abraham did. This is how the mention of Abraham gets into this discussion in the first place. They appeal to Abraham and to their relationship to him in order to deny that they have any need of liberation. Remember that there were many people in Jesus' day who believed that because they were born Jews, they were included in the kingdom of God. Yet not all who were biological descendants of Abraham received the promises God gave to Abraham.

We have the same problem in the church today. You ask, 'Are you a Christian?' and someone may respond, 'Of course

I'm a Christian. I was born a Christian, born into a Christian family, and I go to church.' But no one is born a Christian. No one is automatically in the kingdom of God because their parents are Christians, or because they're members of a church. We must be in Christ to be a Christian. The opponents of Jesus made this same error.

Slaves to sin

I was interviewed once for a series of programmes that were being presented about Reformed theology. The person running the programme asked me what the basic issue was between Reformed theology and historic semi-Pelagianism.[1] I said it comes down to a different understanding of freedom and the will. The principle problem people have with divine sovereignty and election is the idea of man's free will. We are volitional creatures. God has given us minds and hearts and he has given us wills. We exercise that will all the time. We make choices every minute of the day. We choose what we want and we choose freely. No one is coercing us, as if putting a gun to our head. We're not robots; robots don't have minds, wills or hearts. We're human beings and we make choices. That's why we're in trouble with God. The choices we make in our fallen condition are not godly choices. We choose according to our desires, which the Bible tells us are only wicked continuously. We are dead in sins

[1] A weaker form of the heretical teaching of Pelagius, a 5th-century monk, which nevertheless taught that man was not so hopelessly fallen that he could not, of his own free will, cooperate with the grace of God to make salvation effective.—*Ed.*

and trespasses, even though biologically we're alive. We're walking according to the course of this world, according to the prince of the power of the air, fulfilling the lusts of the flesh. This is the clear teaching of Scripture.

The Bible makes it clear that we are actively involved in making choices for which we are responsible and which ultimately expose us to the judgment of God. Yet, at the same time, the Bible teaches us that we're enslaved. We're free from coercion, but we are not free from our own sinful inclinations, appetites and desires. We're slaves to our sinful impulses. That's what the Bible teaches again and again. The humanist doctrine of free will says man is free, not only from coercion, in the sense that his will is indifferent, but also that the will has no predisposition, inclination, bias or bent toward sin because they deny the nature of the fall. The Bible teaches, however, that we are fallen creatures who make decisions, but we make them in the context of our prison of sin. The only way we can get out of that prison is by God setting us free.

This is exactly what the Jewish leaders didn't want to hear. Jesus said, 'Truly, truly, I say to you, everyone who practises sin is a slave to sin. The slave does not remain in the house forever; the son remains forever. So if the Son sets you free, you will be free indeed' (verses 34, 35). Jesus makes another reference here to slavery. Jesus is saying that you may not be a slave necessarily to the Romans or Babylonians, but you're a slave to sin, and it reigns in you. Sin rules in your mortal body.

Children of wrath

The New Testament tells us that we are children of wrath and disobedience by nature. Never are we, by nature, the children of God. The only time we can become the children of God is by adoption because God has only one child. The *monogenēs*, the 'only begotten,' who is Christ. And we find Jesus entering into a dispute with his opponents who claim a special relationship to Abraham, who claim a special relationship to God. Jesus continues this dispute by saying:

> I know that you are offspring of Abraham; yet you seek to kill me because my word finds no place in you. I speak of what I have seen with my Father, and you do what you have heard from your father.' They answered him, 'Abraham is our father.' Jesus said to them, 'If you were Abraham's children, you would be doing the works Abraham did, but now you seek to kill me, a man who has told you the truth that I heard from God. This is not what Abraham did. You are doing the works your father did.' They said to him, 'We were not born of sexual immorality. We have one Father— even God.' Jesus said to them, 'If God were your Father, you would love me, for I came from God and I am here. I came not of my own accord, but he sent me. Why do you not understand what I say? It is because you cannot bear to hear my word. You are of your father the devil' (verses 37-44).

There's a motif throughout Scripture that sonship is measured not simply by biology, but also according to obedience. You are the children of those whom you obey. If you obey Satan, then you're a child of Satan, because sonship is measured by obedience. This is why Jesus says, 'If God were your Father, you would love me, for I came from God and I am here. I came not of my own accord, but he sent me. Why do you not understand what I say? It is because you cannot bear to hear my word' (verses 42, 43).

Remember Jesus says later in John's Gospel, standing before Pilate, 'Everyone who is of the truth listens to my voice' (18:37). Before someone listens to Christ, God has to enable them to listen. Every time I read the Scriptures in church on Sunday morning, I say, 'He who has ears to hear, let him hear.' I do this because I know not everyone has ears to hear. A part of the judgment God gives against sin is to plug the ears of sinful people and put scales over their eyes so that, 'Seeing they do not see, and hearing they do not hear, nor do they understand' (Matt. 13:13). It is only when God, in his grace, stoops to remove those obstacles to hearing and takes away the scales from our eyes that we hear and see. Jesus is acknowledging this truth by affirming that those who don't hear are not able to because God hasn't given them that ability. Instead Jesus tells them, 'You are of your father the devil, and your will is to do your father's desires' (John 8:44). Jesus is talking about their free will. People say today that unless your will is utterly indifferent – has no bent toward good or evil – you're not really free. If that's the case, no one is free. Our wills are passionately motivated by a desire to do the will of the devil.

It's not as if the devil comes in and forces people to obey him. We can't say on the last day, 'Oh, the devil made me do it; he forced me to sin.' No, Jesus says it goes deeper than that. You *desire* to do the will of the devil. You are an eager accomplice to the strategies of Satan. Jesus tells the Pharisees, '[Satan] was a murderer from the beginning, and does not stand in the truth, because there is no truth in him. When he lies, he speaks out of his own character, for he is a liar and the father of lies. But because I tell the truth, you do not believe me' (verses 44, 45).

After telling the Pharisees they are indeed slaves to sin, willing to do the desires of Satan, he demands them to speak up, 'Which one of you convicts me of sin?' (verse 46). I would never say that. I would never challenge anyone to point out the sin in my life, but Jesus does. 'If I tell the truth, why do you not believe me? Whoever is of God hears the words of God. The reason why you do not hear them is that you are not of God' (verses 46, 47). Jesus didn't say that the Pharisees don't hear because they are deaf. He didn't say they don't hear because they are stupid. He said they don't hear because they're not of God. And now the Jews respond:

'Are we not right in saying that you are a Samaritan and have a demon?' Jesus answered, 'I do not have a demon, but I honour my Father, and you dishonour me. Yet I do not seek my own glory; there is One who seeks it, and he is the judge. Truly, truly, I say to you, if anyone keeps my word, he will never see death.' The Jews said to him, 'Now we know that you have a demon! Abraham died, as did the prophets, yet you say, "If anyone keeps my word, he will never taste death." Are you greater than our father Abraham, who died? And the prophets died! Who do you make yourself out to be?' (verses 48-53).

This exchange harks back to chapter 4 of John's Gospel where Jesus has the discussion with the Samaritan woman at the well and she says to him, 'Are you greater than our father Jacob?' (4:12). Yet now instead of sincere questioning, the Jews are challenging him. And Jesus responds:

'If I glorify myself, my glory is nothing. It is my Father who glorifies me, of whom you say, "He is our God." But you have not known him. I know him. If I were to say that I do not know him, I would be a liar like you, but I do know him and I keep his word. Your father Abraham rejoiced that he would see my day. He saw it and was glad.' So the Jews said to him, 'You are not yet fifty years old, and have you seen Abraham?' (8:54-57).

Notice how Jesus responds, 'Truly, truly, I say to you, before Abraham was, I am' (verse 58). Jesus doesn't say, 'Before Abraham was, I was'; he instead uses a term which God utilizes to identify himself. Two thousand years prior to this moment, God the Father gave the promise to Abraham that out of his seed one would come to redeem the world. We don't know the degree to which Abraham understood the content of God's promise, but Abraham believed it and was justified. Jesus is explaining to the Pharisees that when

God spoke to Abraham – whom they claimed to have as their father – God was speaking about Jesus. That is why Abraham rejoiced. Jesus is saying that the Pharisees can't be children of Abraham and oppose him. The initial revelation that God gave to Abraham was a promise being fulfilled by the incarnation of the One who was before Abraham, who was before all creation – the eternal *Logos*, the only begotten Son of the Father. In this exchange we see another reference to the *Logos* concept that John introduced in the very first chapter of his Gospel: 'In the beginning was the Word, and the Word was with God, and the Word was God' (1:1). Jesus is the pre-existent eternal God. This is what Jesus is saying to the Pharisees. 'Before Abraham was, *egō eimi* – I am.'

And the Pharisees didn't miss the significance of what Jesus was saying. This is one of the purest, unvarnished declarations of deity Jesus made during his ministry. His audience did not miss the claim because they tried to kill him: 'So they picked up stones to throw at him, but Jesus hid himself and went out of the temple' (8:59). They wanted to take his life that very moment because they heard in his words a claim to deity.

Jesus is the Eternal One who came to this world as the Bread of Life. He came as the Light of the World. He came as the Door. He came as the Good Shepherd. He came as the Resurrection and the Life. He came as the Way, the Truth, and the Life. He came as the True Vine. And he is the One who, before Abraham was, *Is*.

The Banner of Truth Trust originated in 1957 in London. The founders believed that much of the best literature of historic Christianity had been allowed to fall into oblivion and that, under God, its recovery could well lead not only to a strengthening of the church, but to true revival.

Inter-denominational in vision, this publishing work is now international, and our lists include a number of contemporary authors together with classics from the past. The translation of these books into many languages is encouraged.

A monthly magazine, *The Banner of Truth*, is also published. More information about this and all our publications can be found on our website or supplied by either of the offices below.

THE BANNER OF TRUTH TRUST

3 Murrayfield Road
Edinburgh, EH12 6EL
UK

PO Box 621, Carlisle
Pennsylvania 17013,
USA

www.banneroftruth.org